Common Core ELA Lit

Assessment Prep for Common Core Reading

Grade 7

Tips and Practice for the Reading Standards

Literature • Informational Text • Primary Sources

AUTHORS: SCHYRLET CAMERON and SUZANNE MYERS
EDITORS: MARY DIETERICH and SARAH M. ANDERSON
PROOFREADER: MARGARET BROWN

COPYRIGHT © 2015 Mark Twain Media, Inc.

ISBN 978-1-62223-520-9

Printing No. CD-404224

Mark Twain Media, Inc., Publishers
Distributed by Carson-Dellosa Publishing LLC

Table of Contents

Introduction

Assessment Prep for Common Core Reading, Grade 7 focuses on the Reading standards for English Language Arts (ELA) & Literacy in History/Social Studies, Science, and Technical Subjects. The book is designed to help seventh-grade students acquire the skills and practice the strategies needed to successfully perform on the ELA/Literacy Common Core assessments (online or print).

During the development of the book, we paid special attention to the complexity and word count of literary and informational text excerpts. The text complexity of reading selections will require students to perform close reading. The book is divided into three sections.

◇ The **Test-Taking Tips** section includes tips on preparing for and taking assessments.

◇ The **Instructional Resources** section contains eleven mini-lessons. Each lesson focuses on a different reading comprehension skill, such as making inferences, recognizing point of view, or citing evidence. Each lesson has a short reading passage followed by a sample assessment question. Included in the lesson is a test-taking tip or strategy to help students determine the best way to answer a question.

◇ The **Practice Assessments** section provides students with opportunities to practice their test-taking skills. Each test has a reading selection followed by selected- and constructed-response questions similar to the types of assessment items developed by the testing consortiums. The literature and informational text reading selections cover three types of text: descriptive, expository, and narrative. Some of the text selections are primary sources. This section is divided into three parts.

- **Literature:** includes novel, poem, and drama reading selections

- **Informational Text:** includes speech, autobiography, science article, newspaper article, and flyer (functional text) reading selections

- **Paired Text:** includes two reading selections (primary source and secondary source) on a related topic

A matrix is provided as a quick reference guide for lesson planning. Its purpose is to identify the ELA/Literacy Common Core State Standards addressed in the book.

Common Core State Standards Matrix

English Language Arts Reading Standards

Units of Study	Reading Literature										Reading Informational Text									
	Standard 1	Standard 2	Standard 3	Standard 4	Standard 5	Standard 6	Standard 7	Standard 8	Standard 9	Standard 10	Standard 1	Standard 2	Standard 3	Standard 4	Standard 5	Standard 6	Standard 7	Standard 8	Standard 9	Standard 10
Instructional Resources	X	X		X		X					X	X		X	X	X				
Novel	X	X	X	X	X	X		*		X										
Poem	X	X	X	X	X	X		*		X										
Drama	X		X	X	X	X		*		X										
Speech											X	X		X		X				X
Autobiography											X	X		X	X	X				X
Science Article											X	X		X	X	X	X			X
Newspaper Article											X	X		X		X				X
Flyer (Functional Text)											X			X		X				X
Paired Text											X	X		X	X	X		X	X	X

*This standard is not applicable to literature.

Literacy Standards

Units of Study	Literacy in History/ Social Studies										Literacy in Science & Technical Subjects									
	RH.6-8.1	RH.6-8.2	RH.6-8.3	RH.6-8.4	RH.6-8.5	RH.6-8.6	RH.6-8.7	RH.6-8.8	RH.6-8.9	RH.6-8.10	RST.6-8.1	RST.6-8.2	RST.6-8.3	RST.6-8.4	RST.6-8.5	RST.6-8.6	RST.6-8.7	RST.6-8.8	RST.6-8.9	RST.6-8.10
Speech	X			X		X		X		X										
Autobiography	X			X	X					X										
Science Article											X	X		X	X	X	X	X		X
Newspaper Article	X	X		X		X		X		X										
Paired Text	X	X		X	X	X		X	X	X										

©Copyright 2010. National Governors Association Center for Best Practices and Council of Chief State School Officers. All rights reserved.

Test-Taking Tips

Prepare for Success

During the School Year:

➤ Attend school regularly.

➤ Listen and participate in class.

➤ Ask questions when you don't understand.

➤ Complete homework assignments.

➤ Learn testing vocabulary.

➤ Practice technology skills for online testing.

Before Taking the Test:

➤ Get plenty of sleep the night before testing.

➤ Eat a healthy breakfast the morning of the test.

➤ Go to the restroom before entering the testing room.

➤ Bring needed supplies to the testing room.

Test-Taking Tips

Keys to Success

➤ Be confident and maintain a positive attitude.

➤ Manage your time wisely.

➤ Read or listen to all directions.

➤ Read each question carefully.

➤ Read all answer choices before choosing one.

➤ Eliminate wrong choices, then choose the best answer.

➤ Use details or evidence to support a written response.

➤ Skip or flag difficult questions and answer them last.

➤ Review your answers.

➤ Make sure you have answered all questions.

➤ Think twice before changing an answer.

Test-Taking Tips

Ten Strategies for Success

1. Preview the reading selection for organizational structures and text features.

2. Read all titles, headings, subheadings, maps, charts, graphs, and diagrams carefully.

3. To help you understand the meaning of the text, create mental pictures of what you are reading.

4. As you read, take notes to help you remember and understand key ideas and details.

5. To help you comprehend difficult text, remember to slow down, re-read, or break the text into small chunks.

6. When determining the theme or central idea of a text, the first sentence, the last sentence, or the title usually provides a clue.

7. When you are trying to figure out a vocabulary word from context, replace the word with each of the answer choices and see which answer makes the most sense.

8. Pay close attention to words or phrases in a question that are underlined or are in bold print.

9. Decide what you think the answer to a question is before reading the choices. Then look in order to see if your answer is there.

10. When a question contains the word *best,* remember that there is probably more than one possible answer. You need to look for the **BEST** answer.

Adapted from *Preparing Students for Standardized Testing, Grade 6* by Janet P. Sitter. Used with permission of Mark Twain Media, Inc. Publishers.

Name: _____ Date: _____

Test-Taking Tips
Technology Skills Self-Assessment

Directions: Read the "Checklist of Skills for Online Assessments" chart. Place a checkmark beside the skills that you can successfully perform. Practice the remaining skills until you become proficient.

Checklist of Skills for Online Assessments

	I know how to . . .
	log in to a computer.
	access the test.
	use function buttons.
	navigate through the text.
	play audio/video clips.
	use the vertical scroll bar.
	drag and drop text.
	highlight text.
	select and deselect answers.
	flag questions for later review.
	create and edit responses.
	submit the test.
	exit the test.

Name: _____ Date: _____

Reading Comprehension

Reading comprehension is the ability to understand what you are reading.

 When the text becomes difficult or confusing, remember to slow down, re-read, or break the text into small chunks. Creating a mental picture of what you are reading also helps with comprehension.

Directions: Read the text and answer the sample assessment question.

Text: "The Sun" by Don Powers, Ph.D. and John B. Beaver, Ph.D.

The sun is by far the largest heavenly body near the earth. It is so large that even the largest planets are tiny by comparison. The sun generates its own light, and we depend on that light for many things. Sunlight not only brightens our world but also causes plants to grow and drives the weather processes that bring us winds, clouds, rain, and snow. Without the sun, life on Earth would not be possible. Also, without the sun, we would not be able to see the moon and other planets. The moon and planets do not create their own light. We see them because of the sunlight that reflects off their surfaces.

Although we usually think of our sun as being something special, it is really just an ordinary star. Compared to the rest of the solar system, however, it is something special. The sun contains about 98% of the mass of the solar system and provides almost all of its energy. Its diameter is about 110 times the diameter of the earth.

The center portion, or core, of the sun is a blazing furnace where hydrogen is being converted into helium. The conversion process is the same one that goes on in a hydrogen bomb, and the temperature in the core is a toasty 15 million degrees Celsius! Several layers above the core, energy is transported upward toward the surface of the sun to the part we call the photosphere.

Astronomy: Our Solar System and Beyond by Don Powers, Ph.D., and John B. Beaver, Ph.D. Used with permission of Mark Twain Media, Inc., Publishers

---

Sample Assessment Question

Why is sunlight important to life on Earth? Check all that apply.
- ○ A. "largest heavenly body near the earth"
- ○ B. "generates its own light"
- ○ C. "drives the weather processes"
- ○ D. "causes plants to grow"
- ○ E. "planets do not create their own light"
- ○ F. "core of the sun is a blazing furnace"

Name: _____ Date: _____

Making Inferences

An **inference** is a conclusion based on reasoning and textual evidence. The reader makes an inference when trying to figure out something the author has not stated explicitly in the text.

 To make an inference, use clues from the text and what you already know about the topic.

Directions: Read the text and answer the sample assessment questions.

Text: "Colonial Express Riders" by Cindy Barden

The Boston Committee of Correspondence employed Paul Revere and others as express riders to carry news, messages, and copies of resolutions to other colonies. On the night of April 18, 1775, they sent Paul Revere from Boston to Lexington to warn Samuel Adams and John Hancock that the British were about to arrest them and to alert the militia that troops planned to seize weapons and ammunition stored at Concord. They also sent another rider, William Dawes, by a different route with the same warning. By the end of the night, Revere and Dawes were joined by as many as forty men on horseback spreading the word across Boston's Middlesex County.

Exploration, Revolution, and Constitution by Cindy Barden. Used with permission of Mark Twain Media, Inc., Publishers.

Sample Assessment Questions

Part A
Based upon the text, what can the reader **most likely** infer about express riders?
- ○ A. Express riders played a major role during the American Revolutionary War.
- ○ B. The Boston Committee of Correspondence sent over 40 riders to warn the militia on the night of April 18, 1775.
- ○ C. Express riders were expert horsemen.
- ○ D. Paul Revere alerted the militia that troops planned to seize weapons stored at Concord.

Part B
Highlight **two** details in the text that support the answer in Part A.

Name: _____ Date: _____

Textual Evidence

Textual evidence is the information within the text that supports the author's claim or argument.

 To identify evidence or supporting details, search the text for facts, reasons, and statements that support the claim of the author.

Directions: Read the text and answer the sample assessment question.

Text: Letter to Doctor Walter Jones from Thomas Jefferson (excerpt)

He was, indeed, in every sense of the words, a wise, a good, and a great man.... His person, you know, was fine, his stature exactly what one would wish, his deportment easy, erect, and noble; the best horseman of his age, and the most, graceful figure that could be seen on horseback.... On the whole, his character was, in its mass, perfect, in nothing bad, in few points indifferent; and it may truly be said, that never did nature and fortune combine more perfectly to make a man great, and to place him in the same constellation with whatever worthies have merited from man an everlasting remembrance. For his was the singular destiny and merit, of leading the armies of his country successfully through an arduous war, for the establishment of its independence; of conducting its councils through the birth of a government, new in its forms and principles, until it had settled down into a quiet and orderly train; and of scrupulously obeying the laws through the whole of his career, civil and military, of which the history of the world furnishes no other example....

These are my opinions of General Washington, which I would vouch at the judgment-seat of God, having been formed on an acquaintance of thirty years...

Public Domain

Sample Assessment Question

In his letter, Thomas Jefferson states that, in his opinion, George Washington was "a wise, a good, and a great man."

What are **two** details from the text that show Jefferson's claim is based on sound reasoning?

Write your answer in the box.

Name: _____ Date: _____

Theme

The **theme** is the main message or moral of a story or poem. Some common themes are freedom, survival, friendship, and patriotism.

TIP ▶ To help determine the theme of a text, you must identify its main idea.

Directions: Read the text and answer the sample assessment questions.

Text: "Something Childish, But Very Natural"
by Samuel Taylor Coleridge

If I had but two little wings
And were a little feathery bird,
To you I'd fly, my dear!
But thoughts like these are idle things,
And I stay here.

But in my sleep to you I fly:
I'm always with you in my sleep!
The world is all one's own,
But then one wakes, and where am I?
All, all alone.

Sleep stays not, though a monarch bids:
So I love to wake ere break of day:
For though my sleep be gone,
Yet while 'tis dark, one shuts one's lids,
And still dreams on.

Public Domain

Sample Assessment Questions

Part A
Which statement **best** reflects the theme of the poem?
- ○ A. Dreaming occurs during sleep time.
- ○ B. Dreaming allows wishes to be fulfilled.
- ○ C. Dreaming only occurs at night.
- ○ D. Dreaming is a way to relive childhood.

Part B
Highlight the **two** lines of the poem that provide evidence to support the answer in Part A.

Name: _____ Date: _____

Central Idea

The **central idea** is the most important idea of a text. Nonfiction works may contain multiple central ideas.

 The central or main idea is often revealed by the title or in the first or last sentences of the text. Other times, it is revealed through the key details in the text.

Directions: Read the text and answer the sample assessment question.

Text: "Financing the Government" by Schyrlet Cameron, Janie Doss, and Suzanne Myers

Revenue

The United States government needs a source of revenue or income to pay expenses. Examples of expenses are salaries of elected officials such as the President and members of Congress. Also, it pays the salaries of public employees such as soldiers. The government must pay for public goods and services provided to citizens. Public goods and services include national defense, public health services, and education. The revenue comes from a variety of sources, but taxes provide most of the money the government spends. Taxes are charges collected from individuals and businesses. State and local governments also collect taxes to pay expenses.

The Power to Levy Taxes

Taxes have been a part of United States history since colonial days. Overtaxation was a major reason the colonists fought for independence from Great Britain. When the United States Constitution was written, the founding fathers knew the new nation needed a way to raise money to finance such items as roads and defense. The writers of the Constitution decided to give Congress the power to levy and to collect taxes.

Economic Literacy by Schyrlet Cameron, Janie Doss, and Suzanne Myers. Used with permission of Mark Twain Media, Inc., Publishers.

Sample Assessment Question

Which **two** statements **best** reflect the central ideas of the text?
- ○ A. The United States government needs income to operate.
- ○ B. Individuals and businesses are required to pay taxes.
- ○ C. The government would need money to build roads.
- ○ D. State and local governments have the power to collect taxes.
- ○ E. Taxation was a major reason for the American Revolutionary War.
- ○ F. The Constitution gives Congress the authority to charge and collect taxes.

Name: _____ Date: _____

Summary

A **summary** contains the key points of a text. It should not include the writer's personal feelings, opinions, or prior knowledge of the subject.

 A summary is usually three or four sentences that include the central idea of a text with supporting details.

Directions: Read the text and answer the sample assessment question.

Text: "Caffeine 101" by Anne Davies and Kerry Humes

Caffeine actually affects our brain chemistry. As little as 30 mg of caffeine can have an impact on your brain chemistry and affect your mood and behavior. It only takes a few days of regularly consuming caffeine for our brain chemistry to start expecting the caffeine. Some people can become physically dependent and begin to experience withdrawal symptoms on as little as 100 mg of caffeine per day.

If you consume too much caffeine, your heart may start to race and your muscles may twitch. Caffeine, particularly in higher doses, can cause panic attacks. It can also cause tremors, anxiety, or restless and disconnected thoughts and speech.

If you want to cut down on the amount of caffeine you consume, it's a good idea to decrease by small amounts each day. When a person dramatically decreases the level of caffeine they consume, they can experience withdrawal symptoms, including: headache, fatigue, and difficulty concentrating. When you do cut down on caffeine, your brain chemistry adjusts quite quickly, in a matter of days, so the symptoms don't last long.

Healthy Eating & Exercise by Anne Davies and Kerry Humes. Used with permission of Mark Twain Media, Inc., Publishers.

Sample Assessment Question

Which **two** statements should be included in a summary of the text?
- ○ A. Caffeine has an effect on brain chemistry.
- ○ B. An intake of 30 mg of caffeine can affect a person's mood.
- ○ C. Caffeine can cause muscles to twitch.
- ○ D. Consuming high doses of caffeine can cause panic attacks.
- ○ E. Decreasing the amount of caffeine consumed daily can cause withdrawal symptoms.
- ○ F. Low doses of caffeine can cause headaches.

Name: _____ Date: _____

Word Meaning

As you read, you may encounter unfamiliar words.

TIP Use context clues to help you determine the meaning of an unfamiliar word. The context is the other words, phrases, and sentences that surround the unfamiliar word.

Directions: Read the text and answer the sample assessment question.

Text: "Benjamin Rush" by Victor Hicken

Benjamin Rush was an important man in his time. Raised in Pennsylvania and educated at Princeton and later the University of Edinburgh, he practiced medicine in Philadelphia and taught there in the medical college. As a member of the staff of Pennsylvania Hospital, he became interested in social reform. He established the first free clinic in the United States and later took part in fighting a terrible yellow fever <u>epidemic</u> in Philadelphia. Since nothing was known of the germ theory at that time, Rush thought that the outbreak was caused by spoiled coffee on the wharves of the city. He was closer to the cause than he realized. It is very likely that the imported bags also carried large numbers of mosquitoes that carried yellow fever, and those insects spread the disease.

U.S. History: Inventors, Scientists, Artists, & Authors by Victor Hicken. Used with permission of Mark Twain Media, Inc., Publishers.

Sample Assessment Question

Which **two** words or phrases from the text help the reader determine the meaning of <u>epidemic</u>?
- ○ A. *yellow fever*
- ○ B. *germ theory*
- ○ C. *outbreak*
- ○ D. *spoiled coffee*
- ○ E. *mosquitoes*
- ○ F. *spread the disease*

Name: _____ Date: _____

Tone

Tone is how an author feels toward the topic or subject of the text. Authors create tone by using words with positive or negative connotations. They also use figurative language, such as similes, metaphors, and personification. Examples of words that describe tone are *cheery, angry, amused,* and *sad.*

TIP ▶ Look closely at the author's choice of words. Identify the connotation of words and search for examples of figurative language.

Directions: Read the text and answer the sample assessment questions.

Text: *Call of the Wild* by Jack London

The distance had been measured off, and as he neared the pile of firewood which marked the end of the hundred yards, a cheer began to grow and grow, which burst into a roar as he passed the firewood and halted at command. Every man was tearing himself loose, even Matthewson. Hats and mittens were flying in the air. Men were shaking hands, it did not matter with whom, and bubbling over in a general incoherent babel.

Public Domain

Sample Assessment Questions

Part A
Which word **best** describes the tone of the passage?
- ○ A. happiness
- ○ B. hopeful
- ○ C. joyful
- ○ D. jubilation

Part B
What are **two** details from the text that support the answer in Part A?

Write your answer in the box.

Name: _____ Date: _____

Organizational Text Structures

Text structures are organizational patterns used to break information down into parts that can be easily understood by the reader.

Common Organizational Text Structures

Compare/Contrast	Definition	Classification	Description
examines how concepts and events are alike and different. Signal words/phrases: *alike, different, same, compare to*	introduces and explains a word or concept. Signal words/phrases: *is, for example, also, can be, in fact*	divides topics into related categories or groups. Signal words/phrases: *group, divide, sort, classify, type*	describes something using details and/or examples. Signal words/phrases: *such as, for example, looks like*
Argument/Support	**Cause/Effect**	**Chronological/Sequential**	**Problem/Solution**
states a point of view and supports it with details or evidence. Signal words/phrases: *I believe, in my opinion, I think*	presents a major idea or event and resulting effects. Signal words/phrases: *because of, as a result of, due to, causing*	arranges events in time order or a list of steps in a process. Signal words/phrases: *in, by, later, then, before, finally, first, next, now, after, last*	states a problem and gives possible solutions. Signal words/phrases: *question is, answer is, problem is*

TIP Use signal words and phrases to help identify organizational text structures.

Directions: Read the text and answer the sample assessment question.

Text: "Nonrenewable and Renewable Energy Sources" by Schyrlet Cameron and Carolyn Craig

Most of the world's energy comes from nonrenewable energy sources. These sources are limited and cannot be replaced in a timely manner by natural processes. Most nonrenewable energy is used to make electricity and liquid fuels, such as gasoline. Coal, petroleum, natural gas, propane, and uranium are examples of nonrenewable energy sources. These resources come from the ground.

Alternative Energy Experiments by Schyrlet Cameron and Carolyn Craig. Used with permission of Mark Twain Media, Inc., Publishers

Sample Assessment Question

Which type of structure **best** describes the way the text is organized?

- ○ A. cause/effect
- ○ B. compare/contrast
- ○ C. chronological
- ○ D. description

Name: _____ Date: _____

Author's Purpose

The **author's purpose** is the reason an author writes about a specific topic.

TIP ▶ To determine the author's purpose, ask yourself these questions:

- Did the author try to amuse me? (Entertain)
- Did the author try to teach me about something? (Inform/Explain)
- Did the author try to influence me by giving an opinion? (Persuade)
- Did the author give details to make something clear? (Describe)

Directions: Read the text and answer the sample assessment question.

Text: President John F. Kennedy, May 25, 1961

(The following is an excerpt from a speech delivered by President John F. Kennedy on May 25, 1961, to a joint session of Congress)

I therefore ask the Congress, above and beyond the increases I have earlier requested for space activities, to provide the funds which are needed to meet the following national goals:

First, I believe that this nation should commit itself to achieving the goal, before this decade is out, of landing a man on the moon and returning him safely to the earth. No single space project in this period will be more impressive to mankind, or more important for the long-range exploration of space; and none will be so difficult or expensive to accomplish. We propose to accelerate the development of the appropriate lunar space craft. We propose to develop alternate liquid and solid fuel boosters, much larger than any now being developed, until certain which is superior. We propose additional funds for other engine development and for unmanned explorations—explorations which are particularly important for one purpose which this nation will never overlook: the survival of the man who first makes this daring flight. But in a very real sense, it will not be one man going to the moon—if we make this judgment affirmatively, it will be an entire nation. For all of us must work to put him there.

Public Domain

Sample Assessment Question

What is the author's purpose for writing the text?
- ○ A. to explain the role of the United States in space exploration
- ○ B. to describe the steps in launching a lunar space craft
- ○ C. to persuade Congress to approve additional funding for space exploration
- ○ D. to entertain U.S. citizens with stories about space exploration

Name: _____ Date: _____

Point of View

Point of view is the perspective from which something is written or told. Depending on the type of writing, the point of view expresses the thoughts, feelings, and beliefs of a narrator, character, author, or speaker.

 To help identify the point of view, look at the personal pronouns used in the text. Words like *I* and *we* are used with **first-person** point of view. Words like *he, she,* and *it* help to identify **third-person** point of view.

Directions: Read the text and answer the sample assessment question.

Text: *The Jungle Book* by Rudyard Kipling

"How little! How naked, and—how bold!" said Mother Wolf softly. The baby was pushing his way between the cubs to get close to the warm hide. "Ahai! He is taking his meal with the others. And so this is a man's cub. Now, was there ever a wolf that could boast of a man's cub among her children?"

"I have heard now and again of such a thing, but never in our Pack or in my time," said Father Wolf. "He is altogether without hair, and I could kill him with a touch of my foot. But see, he looks up and is not afraid."

The moonlight was blocked out of the mouth of the cave, for Shere Khan's great square head and shoulders were thrust into the entrance. Tabaqui, behind him, was squeaking: "My lord, my lord, it went in here!"

"Shere Khan does us great honor," said Father Wolf, but his eyes were very angry. "What does Shere Khan need?"

"My quarry. A man's cub went this way," said Shere Khan. "Its parents have run off. Give it to me."

Public Domain

Sample Assessment Question

Which **best** describes the point of view used in the text?
- ○ A. first-person from Mother Wolf's point of view
- ○ B. first-person from Shere Khan's point of view
- ○ C. third-person from Father Wolf's point of view
- ○ D. third-person from the narrator's point of view

Name: _____ Date: _____

Novel

Directions: Read the text and answer the questions.

Text: *The Secret Garden* by Frances Hodgson Burnett

In each century since the beginning of the world wonderful things have been discovered. In the last century more amazing things were found out than in any century before. In this new century hundreds of things still more astounding will be brought to light. At first people refuse to believe that a strange new thing can be done, then they begin to hope it can be done, then they see it can be done—then it is done and all the world wonders why it was not done centuries ago. One of the new things people began to find out in the last century was that thoughts—just mere thoughts—are as powerful as electric batteries—as good for one as sunlight is, or as bad for one as poison. To let a sad thought or a bad one get into your mind is as dangerous as letting a scarlet fever germ get into your body. If you let it stay there after it has got in you may never get over it as long as you live...

While the secret garden was coming alive and two children were coming alive with it, there was a man wandering about certain far-away beautiful places in the Norwegian fiords and the valleys and mountains of Switzerland and he was a man who for ten years had kept his mind filled with dark and heart-broken thinking. He had not been courageous; he had never tried to put any other thoughts in the place of the dark ones. He had wandered by blue lakes and thought them; he had lain on mountain-sides with sheets of deep blue gentians blooming all about him and flower breaths filling all the air and he had thought them. A terrible sorrow had fallen upon him when he had been happy and he had let his soul fill itself with blackness and had refused obstinately to allow any rift of light to pierce through. He had forgotten and deserted his home and his duties. When he traveled about, darkness so brooded over him that the sight of him was a wrong done to other people because it was as if he poisoned the air about him with gloom. Most strangers thought he must be either half mad or a man with some hidden crime on his soul. He was a tall man with a drawn face and crooked shoulders and the name he always entered on hotel registers was, "Archibald Craven, Misselthwaite Manor, Yorkshire, England."

He had traveled far and wide since the day he saw Mistress Mary in his study and told her she might have her "bit of earth." He had been in the most beautiful places in Europe, though he had remained nowhere more than a few days. He had chosen the quietest and remotest spots. He had been on the tops of mountains whose heads were in the clouds and had looked down on other mountains when the sun rose and touched them with such light as made it seem as if the world were just being born.

But the light had never seemed to touch himself until one day when he realized that for the first time in ten years a strange thing had happened. He was in a wonderful valley in the Austrian Tyrol and he had been walking alone through such beauty as might have lifted any man's soul out of shadow. He had

Name: _____ Date: _____

Novel (cont.)

walked a long way and it had not lifted his. But at last he had felt tired and had thrown himself down to rest on a carpet of moss by a stream. It was a clear little stream which ran quite merrily along on its narrow way through the luscious damp greenness. Sometimes it made a sound rather like very low laughter as it bubbled over and round stones. He saw birds come and dip their heads to drink in it and then flick their wings and fly away. It seemed like a thing alive and yet its tiny voice made the stillness seem deeper. The valley was very, very still.

As he sat gazing into the clear running of the water, Archibald Craven gradually felt his mind and body both grow quiet, as quiet as the valley itself. He wondered if he were going to sleep, but he was not. He sat and gazed at the sunlit water and his eyes began to see things growing at its edge. There was one lovely mass of blue forget-me-nots growing so close to the stream that its leaves were wet and at these he found himself looking as he remembered he had looked at such things years ago. He was actually thinking tenderly how lovely it was and what wonders of blue its hundreds of little blossoms were. He did not know that just that simple thought was slowly filling his mind—filling and filling it until other things were softly pushed aside. It was as if a sweet clear spring had begun to rise in a stagnant pool and had risen and risen until at last it swept the dark water away. But of course he did not think of this himself. He only knew that the valley seemed to grow quieter and quieter as he sat and stared at the bright delicate blueness. He did not know how long he sat there or what was happening to him, but at last he moved as if he were awakening and he got up slowly and stood on the moss carpet, drawing a long, deep, soft breath and wondering at himself. Something seemed to have been unbound and released in him, very quietly.

"What is it?" he said, almost in a whisper, and he passed his hand over his forehead. "I almost feel as if—I were alive!"

I do not know enough about the wonderfulness of undiscovered things to be able to explain how this had happened to him. Neither does any one else yet. He did not understand at all himself—but he remembered this strange hour months afterward when he was at Misselthwaite again and he found out quite by accident that on this very day Colin had cried out as he went into the secret garden:

"I am going to live forever and ever and ever!"

The singular calmness remained with him the rest of the evening and he slept a new reposeful sleep; but it was not with him very long. He did not know that it could be kept. By the next night he had opened the doors wide to his dark thoughts and they had come trooping and rushing back. He left the valley and went on his wandering way again. But, strange as it seemed to him, there were minutes—sometimes half-hours—when, without his knowing why, the black burden seemed to lift itself again and he knew he was a living man and not a dead one. Slowly—slowly—for no reason that he knew of—he was "coming alive" with the garden.

Name: _____ Date: _____

Novel (cont.)

Assessment Questions

1. Read the sentence from the text and the directions that follow.

> He had wandered by blue lakes and thought them; he had lain on mountain-sides with sheets of deep blue <u>gentians</u> blooming all about him and flower breaths filling all the air and he had thought them.

   Select the meaning of the word <u>gentians</u> as it is used in the sentence.
   - ○ A. dark shade of blue
   - ○ B. type of flower
   - ○ C. covering for a bed
   - ○ D. algae found in lakes

2. **Part A**
   Choose **one** word that describes Archibald Craven's personality as revealed through the text. There is more than one correct choice.
   - ○ A. content
   - ○ B. serious
   - ○ C. steadfast
   - ○ D. stubborn
   - ○ E. irresponsible
   - ○ F. gloomy

   Part B
   Which **two** details from the text **best** supports the answer chosen in Part A?
   - ○ A. "never tried to put any other thoughts in the place of the dark ones"
   - ○ B. "felt his mind and body both grow quiet"
   - ○ C. "darkness so brooded over him"
   - ○ D. "refused obstinately to allow any rift of light to pierce through"
   - ○ E. "kept his mind filled with dark and heart-broken thinking"
   - ○ F. "forgotten and deserted his home and his duties"

3. What is the **main** purpose for the second paragraph of the text?
   - ○ A. to describe the places visited by Archibald Craven
   - ○ B. to explain the connection between Archibald Craven, the children, and the secret garden
   - ○ C. to provide a physical and emotional description of Archibald Craven
   - ○ D. to reveal the location of the Secret Garden

Name: _____ Date: _____

Novel (cont.)

4. Read the excerpt from the text and answer the question.

> He did not know that just that simple thought was slowly filling his mind—
> filling and filling it until other things were softly pushed aside. It was as if a
> sweet clear spring had begun to rise in a stagnant pool and had risen and
> risen until at last it swept the dark water away.

   What was the author's purpose for the use of imagery?
   ○ A. to reveal the darkness of Craven's thoughts
   ○ B. to illustrate how Craven's way of thinking changed
   ○ C. to compare Craven's thoughts to a stagnant pool
   ○ D. to make a comparison between the spring and a stagnant pool

5. Read the excerpt from the text and the directions that follow.

> It was a clear little stream which ran quite merrily along on its narrow way
> through the luscious damp greenness. Sometimes it made a sound rather
> like very low laughter as it bubbled over and round stones. He saw birds
> come and dip their heads to drink in it and then flick their wings and fly away.
> It seemed like a thing alive and yet its tiny voice made the stillness seem
> deeper.

   Personification is giving human-like characteristics to an animal, non-living
   object, or an idea. Select **three** details from the excerpt that reveals the
   author's use of personification in the excerpt.
   ○ A. "a clear little stream"
   ○ B. "ran quite merrily along"
   ○ C. "through the luscious damp greenness"
   ○ D. "it made a sound rather like very low laughter"
   ○ E. "birds come and dip their heads to drink in it"
   ○ F. "flick their wings and fly away"
   ○ G. "its tiny voice made the stillness seem deeper"

6. Which sentence from the text supports the idea that the change in Archibald
   Craven's thoughts was temporary?
   ○ A. "He only knew that the valley seemed to grow quieter and quieter as he
         sat and stared at the bright delicate blueness."
   ○ B. "Something seemed to have been unbound and released in him, very
         quietly."
   ○ C. "I do not know enough about the wonderfulness of undiscovered things
         to be able to explain how this had happened to him."
   ○ D. "By the next night he had opened the doors wide to his dark thoughts
         and they had come trooping and rushing back."

Name: _____ Date: _____

Novel (cont.)

7. Read the excerpt from the text and answer the question.

> He was actually thinking tenderly how lovely it was and what wonders of blue its hundreds of little blossoms were. He did not know that just that simple thought was slowly filling his mind—filling and filling it until other things were softly pushed aside. It was as if a sweet clear spring had begun to rise in a stagnant pool and had risen and risen until at last it swept the dark water away.

Which point of view is used in the excerpt?
- ○ A. The narrator describes his own thoughts and feelings.
- ○ B. The narrator describes Archibald Craven's thoughts and feelings.
- ○ C. Archibald Craven describes the children's thoughts and feelings.
- ○ D. Archibald Craven describes his own thoughts and feelings.

8. Read the statement and follow the directions.

> For ten years, Archibald Craven did not allow positive thoughts to penetrate his being.

Select **two** details from the text that **best** support the statement.
- ○ A. "gradually felt his mind and body both grow quiet"
- ○ B. "he had not been courageous"
- ○ C. "he had never tried to put any other thoughts in the place of the dark ones"
- ○ D. "he had been walking alone through such beauty as might have lifted, any man's soul out of shadow"
- ○ E. "terrible sorrow had fallen upon him when he had been happy"
- ○ F. "he had let his soul fill itself with blackness and had refused obstinately to allow any rift of light to pierce through"

9. Which statement **best** reflects the theme of the text?
- ○ A. A single event can change a person's perspective.
- ○ B. The beauty of mountains inspire positive thinking.
- ○ C. Many people prefer to travel alone.
- ○ D. The sounds of nature are soothing to a person's soul.

10. Which statement would **most likely** be included in a summary of the text?
- ○ A. Archibald Craven allowed sorrow to fill his mind with dark thoughts.
- ○ B. Mistress Mary talked with Archibald Craven in his study.
- ○ C. Archibald Craven saw the mountains in Switzerland.
- ○ D. Archibald Craven enjoyed sitting by the lake looking at the flowers.

Name: _____ Date: _____

Novel (cont.)

11. Read Excerpt 1 and Excerpt 2 from the text and the directions that follow.

Excerpt 1

He did not know how long he sat there or what was happening to him, but at last he moved as if he were awakening and he got up slowly and stood on the moss carpet, drawing a long, deep, soft breath and wondering at himself. Something seemed to have been unbound and released in him, very quietly.

"What is it?" he said, almost in a whisper, and he passed his hand over his forehead. "I almost feel as if—I were alive!"

Excerpt 2

I do not know enough about the wonderfulness of undiscovered things to be able to explain how this had happened to him. Neither does any one else yet. He did not understand at all himself—but he remembered this strange hour months afterward when he was at Misselthwaite again and he found out quite by accident that on this very day Colin had cried out as he went into the secret garden:

"I am going to live forever and ever and ever!"

Explain how Excerpt 2 contributes to your understanding of Excerpt 1. Use evidence from the text to support your answer.

Write your answer in the box.

Name: _____ Date: _____

Poem

Directions: Read the text and answer the questions.

Text: "The Rainy Day" by Henry Wadsworth Longfellow

> The day is cold, and dark, and dreary;
> It rains, and the wind is never weary;
> The vine still clings to the mouldering wall,
> But at every gust the dead leaves fall,
> And the day is dark and dreary!
>
> My life is cold, and dark, and dreary;
> It rains, and the wind is never weary;
> My thoughts still cling to the mouldering past,
> But the hopes of youth fall thick in the blast,
> And the days are dark and dreary.
>
> Be still, sad heart! and cease repining;
> Behind the clouds is the sun still shining;
> Thy fate is the common fate of all,
> Into each life some rain must fall,
> Some days must be dark and dreary.

Public Domain

Assessment Questions

1. Which **two** lines from the poem **most likely** suggest that the speaker is an older person?
   - ○ A. *The vine still clings to the mouldering wall,*
   - ○ B. *But at every gust the dead leaves fall,*
   - ○ C. *My thoughts still cling to the mouldering past,*
   - ○ D. *But the hopes of youth fall thick in the blast,*
   - ○ E. *Thy fate is the common fate of all,*
   - ○ F. *Into each life some rain must fall,*

2. Which phrase from the poem is an example of the poet's use of imagery?
   - ○ A. *dead leaves fall*
   - ○ B. *life is cold*
   - ○ C. *hopes of youth*
   - ○ D. *cease repining*

Name: _____ Date: _____

Poem (cont.)

3. **Part A**
Which word **best** describes the theme of the poem?
   - ○ A. despair
   - ○ B. hope
   - ○ C. rain
   - ○ D. youth

   Part B
   Which line from the poem is the **most** helpful in understanding the theme?
   - ○ A. *It rains, and the wind is never weary;*
   - ○ B. *But the hopes of youth fall thick in the blast,*
   - ○ C. *Behind the clouds is the sun still shining;*
   - ○ D. *Thy fate is the common fate of all,*

4. Based upon stanza two, what generalization can the reader make about the speaker's personality?
   - ○ A. The speaker is pessimistic.
   - ○ B. The speaker is optimistic.
   - ○ C. The speaker is sentimental.
   - ○ D. The speaker is judgmental.

5. Read the line from the poem and answer the question.

   Be still, sad heart! and <u>cease</u> *repining;*

   Which word is the **best** synonym for <u>cease</u> as it is used in the line?
   - ○ A. conclude
   - ○ B. expire
   - ○ C. finish
   - ○ D. stop

6. Alliteration is the repetition of a consonant sound at the beginning of a series of words. Which line from the poem contains an alliteration?
   - ○ A. *But at every gust the dead leaves fall,*
   - ○ B. *But the hopes of youth fall thick in the blast,*
   - ○ C. *Into each life some rain must fall,*
   - ○ D. *Some days must be dark and dreary.*

7. What is **most likely** the poet's purpose for writing the poem?
   - ○ A. to inform the reader that a rainy day is dark and dreary
   - ○ B. to persuade the reader to remain hopeful during times of hardship
   - ○ C. to inform the reader about the effects of grieving on the human body
   - ○ D. to entertain readers with a poem about staying inside on rainy days

Name: _____ Date: _____

Poem (cont.)

8. **Part A**
What is the speaker describing in stanza one?
○ A. life
○ B. plants
○ C. rain
○ D. weather

Part B
Which words or phrases from the poem support the answer in Part A? Select all that apply.
○ A. *day is cold*
○ B. *rains*
○ C. *wind*
○ D. *vine*
○ E. *mouldering wall*
○ F. *dead leaves*

9. Explain how the tone of the poem changes in stanza three. Use evidence from the poem to support your answer.

Write your answer in the box.

Name: _____ Date: _____

Drama

Directions: Read the text and answer the questions.

Text: "Alice in Wonderland, A Dramatization of Lewis Carroll's *Alice's Adventures in Wonderland* and *Through the Looking Glass*" by Alice Gerstenberg

ACT I
SCENE TWO

SETTING: *In Scene Two the portieres are black and red squares like a chessboard. A soft radiance follows the characters mysteriously.*

CURTAIN RISE: *A*LICE *comes through the looking glass; steps down, looks about in wonderment and goes to see if there is a "fire." The* R*ED* Q*UEEN* *rises out of the grate and faces her haughtily.*

ALICE: Why, you're the Red Queen!

RED **Q**UEEN: Of course I am! Where do you come from? And where are you going? Look up, speak nicely, and don't twiddle your fingers!

ALICE: I only wanted to see what the looking glass was like. Perhaps I've lost my way.

RED **Q**UEEN: I don't know what you mean by your way; all the ways about here belong to me. Curtsey while you're thinking what to say. It saves time.

ALICE: I'll try it when I go home; the next time I'm a little late for dinner.

RED **Q**UEEN: [*looking at her watch*] It's time for you to answer now; open your mouth a little wider when you speak, and always say, "Your Majesty." I suppose you don't want to lose your name?

ALICE: No, indeed.

RED **Q**UEEN: And yet I don't know, only think how convenient it would be if you could manage to go home without it! For instance, if the governess wanted to call you to your lessons, she would call out "come here," and there she would have to leave off, because there wouldn't be any name for her to call, and of course you wouldn't have to go, you know.

ALICE: That would never do, I'm sure; the governess would never think of excusing me from lessons for that. If she couldn't remember my name, she'd call me "Miss," as the servants do. [*A*LICE *picks up a book that is lying on a table.*]

RED **Q**UEEN: Well, if she said "Miss," and didn't say anything more, of course you'd miss your lessons. I dare say you can't even read this book.

ALICE: It's all in some language I don't know. Why, it's a looking-glass book, of course! And if I hold it up to a glass, the words will all go the right way again.

Name: _____ Date: _____

Drama (cont.)

JABBERWOCKY
'Twas brillig, and the slithy toves
Did gyre and gimble in the wabe;
All mimsy were the borogoves,
And the mome raths outgrabe.

It seems very pretty, but it's rather hard to understand; somehow it seems to fill my head with ideas—only I don't exactly know what they are.

RED QUEEN: I daresay you don't know your geography either. Look at the map! [*She takes a right angle course to the portieres and points to them with her scepter.*]

ALICE: It's marked out just like a big chessboard. I wouldn't mind being a pawn, though of course I should like to be a Red Queen best.

RED QUEEN: That's easily managed. When you get to the eighth square you'll be a Queen. It's a huge game of chess that's being played—all over the world. Come on, we've got to run. Faster, don't try to talk.

ALICE: I can't.

RED QUEEN: Faster, faster.

ALICE: Are we nearly there?

RED QUEEN: Nearly there! Why, we passed it ten minutes ago. Faster. You may rest a little now.

ALICE: Why, I do believe we're in the same place. Everything's just as it was.

RED QUEEN: Of course it is, what would you have it?

ALICE: Well, in our country you'd generally get to somewhere else—if you ran very fast for a long time as we've been doing.

RED QUEEN: A slow sort of country. Now here you see, it takes all the running you can do, to keep in the same place. If you want to get somewhere else, you must run at least twice as fast as that.

ALICE: I'd rather not try, please! I'm quite content to stay here—only I am so hot and thirsty.

RED QUEEN: I know what you'd like. [*She takes a little box out of her pocket.*] Have a biscuit?

[*ALICE, not liking to refuse, curtseys as she takes the biscuit and chokes.*]

RED QUEEN: While you're refreshing yourself, I'll just take the measurements. [*She takes a ribbon out of her pocket and measures the map with it.*] At the end of two yards I shall give you your directions—have another biscuit?

Name: _____ Date: _____

Drama (cont.)

ALICE: No thank you, one's QUITE enough.

RED QUEEN: Thirst quenched, I hope? At the end of three yards I shall repeat them—for fear of your forgetting them. At the end of four, I shall say good-bye. And at the end of five, I shall go!

[*RED QUEEN turns and faces ALICE*]

RED QUEEN: A pawn goes two squares in its first move, you know. So you'll go very quickly through the Third Square—by railway, I should think—and you'll find yourself in the Fourth Square in no time. Well, that Square belongs to Tweedledum and Tweedledee—the Fifth is mostly water—The Sixth belongs to Humpty Dumpty and that Square to the Gryphon and Mock Turtle and that Square to the Queen of Hearts. But you make no remark?

ALICE: I—I didn't know I had to make one—just then.

RED QUEEN: You should have said, "It's extremely kind of you to tell me all this"—however, we'll suppose it said. [*Alice curtseys.*]

RED QUEEN: Four! Good-bye! Five! [*RED QUEEN vanishes in a gust of wind behind the portieres.*]

[*Rabbit music. WHITE RABBIT comes out of the fireplace and walks about the room hurriedly. He wears a checked coat, carries white kid gloves in one hand, a fan in the other and takes out his watch to look at it anxiously.*]

WHITE RABBIT: Oh the Duchess! The Duchess! Oh, won't she be savage if I've kept her waiting!

ALICE: I've never seen a rabbit with a waistcoat and a watch! And a waistcoat pocket! If you please, sir—

WHITE RABBIT: Oh! [*He drops fan and gloves in fright and dashes out by way of the portieres in a gust of wind. ALICE picks up the fan and playfully puts on the gloves....*]

---

portieres – curtain hanging over a doorway

scepter – an ornamental staff carried by a monarch

Public Domain

Name: _____ Date: _____

Drama (cont.)

Assessment Questions

1. Read the lines of dialogue and answer the question.

> **ALICE:** I'd rather not try, please! I'm quite content to stay here—only I am so hot and thirsty.
>
> **RED QUEEN:** I know what you'd like. [*She takes a little box out of her pocket.*] Have a biscuit?
>
> [*ALICE, not liking to refuse, curtseys as she takes the biscuit and chokes.*]
>
> **RED QUEEN:** While you're refreshing yourself, I'll just take the measurements. [*She takes a ribbon out of her pocket and measures the map with it.*] At the end of two yards I shall give you your directions—have another biscuit?

What is ironic about the Red Queen offering Alice a biscuit?
- ○ A. The Red Queen offers Alice a biscuit out of courtesy.
- ○ B. The Red Queen offers Alice a biscuit to quench her thirst.
- ○ C. The Red Queen offers Alice a biscuit to satisfy her hunger.
- ○ D. The Red Queen offers Alice a biscuit to stop her complaining.

2. Based on the text, which player does Alice desire to be in the "huge game of chess"?
- ○ A. Red Queen
- ○ B. Mock Turtle
- ○ C. Queen of Hearts
- ○ D. White Rabbit

3. Read the lines from the play and answer the question

> **RED QUEEN:** Of course I am! Where do you come from? And where are you going? Look up, speak nicely, and don't twiddle your fingers!

What is the author **most likely** trying to reveal about the Red Queen?
- ○ A. She likes to ask questions and expects an immediate answer.
- ○ B. She expects people to be courteous when speaking.
- ○ C. She has a demanding and overbearing personality.
- ○ D. She expects people to look her in the eye when she is speaking.

4. Read the lines of dialogue from the play and answer the question.

> **ALICE:** Well, in our country you'd generally get to somewhere else—if you ran very fast for a long time as we've been doing.

Name: _____ Date: _____

Drama (cont.)

> **RED QUEEN:** A slow sort of country. Now here you see, it takes all the running you can do, to keep in the same place. If you want to get somewhere else, you must run at least twice as fast as that.

What is **most likely** the playwright's purpose for including the lines?
- A. The author is revealing the Red Queen's opinion of Alice's country.
- B. The author is making a comparison between Alice's world and Wonderland.
- C. The author is revealing Alice's preference for her own country.
- D. The author is emphasizing the rudeness of the Red Queen.

5. Why is the CURTAIN RISE section of the script important?
- A. It gives the reader a description of who and what will be on stage when an act or scene begins.
- B. It lets the characters know where they will be standing when the curtain rises.
- C. It helps the reader to recognize the main characters in the play.
- D. It summarizes what is going to happen during the scene.

6. A stage direction is a written instruction to the actor. Based upon the play, which stage direction would **most likely** be added to Alice's line, "I've never seen a rabbit with a waistcoat and a watch! And a waistcoat pocket! If you please, sir—"?
- A. [*looks amused*]
- B. [*looks puzzled*]
- C. [*sounds pleased*]
- D. [*speaks excitedly*]

7. Read the lines of dialogue from the play and answer the question.

> **RED QUEEN:** And yet I don't know, only think how convenient it would be if you could manage to go home without it! For instance, if the governess wanted to call you to your lessons, she would call out "come here," and there she would have to leave off, because there wouldn't be any name for her to call, and of course you wouldn't have to go, you know.

Which word is the **best** synonym for the word governess as it is used in the line?
- A. babysitter
- B. mother
- C. servant
- D. teacher

Name: _____ Date: _____

Drama (cont.)

8. Read the lines of dialogue from the play and answer the question.

> **RED QUEEN:** While you're refreshing yourself, I'll just take the measurements. [*She takes a ribbon out of her pocket and measures the map with it.*] At the end of two yards I shall give you your directions—have another biscuit?
>
> **ALICE:** No thank you, one's <u>QUITE</u> enough.

Why did the playwright **most likely** write the word <u>QUITE</u> in all capital letters?
- ○ A. The playwright is signaling a change in the character's mood.
- ○ B. The playwright is using the word to reveal the tone of the dialogue.
- ○ C. The playwright wants the actor to shout when speaking the word.
- ○ D. The playwright wants the actor to emphasize the word when speaking the line.

9. What does the playwright reveal about Alice's personality through the stage directions? Support your answer with textual evidence.

Write your answer in the box.

Name: _____ Date: _____

Speech

Directions: Read the speech and answer the questions.

Text: Speech Delivered in the Senate of the United States, March 7, 1850
        by Daniel Webster

For the preservation of the Union.

Mr. President,—I wish to speak to-day, not as a Massachusetts man, nor as a Northern man, but as an American, and a member of the Senate of the United States. It is fortunate that there is a Senate of the United States; a body not yet moved from its propriety, not lost to a just sense of its own dignity and its own high responsibilities, and a body to which the country looks, with confidence, for wise, moderate, patriotic, and healing counsels. It is not to be denied that we live in the midst of strong agitations, and are surrounded by very considerable dangers to our institutions and government. The imprisoned winds are let loose. The East, the North, and the stormy South combine to throw the whole sea into commotion, to toss its billows to the skies, and disclose its profoundest depths. I do not affect to regard myself, Mr. President, as holding, or as fit to hold, the helm in this combat with the political elements; but I have a duty to perform, and I mean to perform it with fidelity, not without a sense of existing dangers, but not without hope. I have a part to act, not for my own security or safety, for I am looking out for no fragment upon which to float away from the wreck, if wreck there must be, but for the good of the whole, and the preservation of all; and there is that which will keep me to my duty during this struggle, whether the sun and the stars shall appear, or shall not appear, for many days. I speak to-day for the preservation of the Union. "Hear me for my cause." I speak to-day, out of a solicitous and anxious heart, for the restoration to the country of that quiet and that harmony which make the blessings of this Union so rich, and so dear to us all. These are the topics that I propose to myself to discuss; these are the motives, and the sole motives, that influence me in the wish to communicate my opinions to the Senate and the country; and if I can do anything, however little, for the promotion of these ends, I shall have accomplished all that I expect...

Peaceable secession impossible.

Mr. President, I should much prefer to have heard from every member on this floor declarations of opinion that this Union could never be dissolved, than the declaration of opinion by anybody that, in any case, under the pressure of any circumstances, such a dissolution was possible. I hear with distress and anguish the word "secession," especially when it falls from the lips of those who are patriotic, and known to the country, and known all over the world, for their political services. Secession! Peaceable secession! Sir, your eyes and mine are never destined to see that miracle. The dismemberment of this vast country without convulsion! The breaking up of the fountains of the great deep without ruffling the surface! Who is so foolish—I beg everybody's pardon—as to expect to see any such thing? Sir, he

Speech (cont.)

who sees these States now revolving in harmony around a common centre, and expects to see them quit their places and fly off without convulsion, may look the next hour to see the heavenly bodies rush from their spheres, and jostle against each other in the realms of space, without causing the wreck of the universe. There can be no such thing as a peaceable secession. Peaceable secession is an utter impossibility. Is the great Constitution under which we live, covering this whole country,—is it to be thawed and melted away by secession, as the snows on the mountain melt under the influence of a vernal sun, disappear almost unobserved, and run off? No, Sir! No, Sir! I will not state what might produce the disruption of the Union; but, Sir, I see as plainly as I see the sun in heaven what that disruption itself must produce; I see that it must produce war, and such a war as I will not describe, in its twofold character.

Peaceable secession! Peaceable secession! The concurrent agreement of all the members of this great republic to separate? A voluntary separation, with alimony on one side and on the other! Why, what would be the result? Where is the line to be drawn? What States are to secede? What is to remain American? What am I to be? An American no longer? Am I to become a sectional man, a local man, a separatist, with no country in common with the gentlemen who sit around me here, or who fill the other house of Congress? Heaven forbid! Where is the flag of the republic to remain? Where is the eagle still to tower? or is he to cower, and shrink, and fall to the ground? Why, Sir, our ancestors, our fathers and our grandfathers, those of them that are yet living amongst us with prolonged lives, would rebuke and reproach us; and our children and our grandchildren would cry out shame upon us, if we of this generation should dishonor these ensigns of the power of the government and the harmony of that Union which is every day felt among us with so much joy and gratitude. What is to become of the army? What is to become of the navy? What is to become of the public lands? How is each of the thirty States to defend itself?

The idea of a Southern Confederacy.

I know, although the idea has not been stated distinctly, there is to be, or it is supposed possible that there will be, a Southern Confederacy. I do not mean, when I allude to this statement, that any one seriously contemplates such a state of things. I do not mean to say that it is true, but I have heard it suggested elsewhere that the idea has been entertained, that, after the dissolution of this Union, a Southern Confederacy might be formed. I am sorry, Sir, that it has ever been thought of, talked of, or dreamed of, in the wildest flights of human imagination. But the idea, so far as it exists, must be of a separation assigning the slave States to one side and the free States to the other. Sir, I may express myself too strongly, perhaps, but there are impossibilities in the natural as well as in the physical world, and I hold the idea of a separation of these States, those that are free to form one government, and those that are slave holding to form another, as such

Speech (cont.)

an impossibility. We could not separate the States by any such line, if we were to draw it. We could not sit down here to-day and draw a line of separation that would satisfy any five men in the country. There are natural causes that would keep and tie us together, and there are social and domestic relations which we could not break if we would, and which we should not if we could.

Liberty and Union.

Instead of speaking of the possibility or utility of secession, instead of dwelling in those caverns of darkness, instead of groping with those ideas so full of all that is horrid and horrible, let us come out into the light of day; let us enjoy the fresh air of Liberty and Union; let us cherish those hopes which belong to us; let us devote ourselves to those great objects that are fit for our consideration and our action; let us raise our conceptions to the magnitude and the importance of the duties that devolve upon us; let our comprehension be as broad as the country for which we act, our aspirations as high as its certain destiny; let us not be pygmies in a case that calls for men. Never did there devolve on any generation of men higher trusts than now devolve upon us, for the preservation of this Constitution and the harmony and peace of all who are destined to live under it. Let us make our generation one of the strongest and brightest links in that golden chain which is destined, I fondly believe, to grapple the people of all the States to this Constitution for ages to come. We have a great popular, constitutional government, guarded by law and by judicature, and defended by the affections of the whole people. No monarchical throne presses these States together, no iron chain of military power encircles them; they live and stand under a government popular in its form, representative in its character, founded upon principles of equality, and so constructed, we hope, as to last forever. In all its history it has been beneficent; it has trodden down no man's liberty; it has crushed no State. Its daily respiration is liberty and patriotism; its yet youthful veins are full of enterprise, courage, and honorable love of glory and renown. Large before, the country has now, by recent events, become vastly larger. This republic now extends, with a vast breadth, across the whole continent. The two great seas of the world wash the one and the other shore. We realize, on a mighty scale, the beautiful description of the ornamental border of the buckler of Achilles:—

"Now, the broad shield complete, the artist crowned
With his last hand, and poured the ocean round;
In living silver seemed the waves to roll,
And beat the buckler's verge, and bound the whole."

Speech (cont.)

Assessment Questions

1. **Part A**
   What is the theme of the speech?
   ○ A. formation of a Southern Confederacy
   ○ B. dissolution of the Union
   ○ C. secession of the southern states
   ○ D. preservation of the Union

   Part B
   Select **two** sentences from the speech that **best** support the answer in Part A.
   ○ A. "We have a great popular, constitutional government, guarded by law and by judicature, and defended by the affections of the whole people."
   ○ B. "I speak to-day for the preservation of the Union."
   ○ C. "...after the dissolution of this Union, a Southern Confederacy might be formed ... ."
   ○ D. "I should much prefer to have heard from every member on this floor declarations of opinion that this Union could never be dissolved, ..."
   ○ E. "Where is the flag of the republic to remain?"
   ○ F. "We could not sit down here to-day and draw a line of separation that would satisfy any five men in the country ... ."

2. What is the **main** purpose of Daniel Webster's speech?
   ○ A. to encourage the audience to support a peaceable succession
   ○ B. to explain to the audience the impossibility of peaceable succession
   ○ C. to persuade the audience to preserve the Union and work together in harmony
   ○ D. to inform the audience about the military's plan to separate free and slave-holding states

3. Who is the intended audience for the speech?
   ○ A. Mr. President
   ○ B. United States Senate
   ○ C. Citizens of Massachusetts
   ○ D. Southern Confederacy

4. Based on the text, how does Daniel Webster describe himself?
   ○ A. American
   ○ B. Northern man
   ○ C. separatist
   ○ D. man with no country

Name: _____ Date: _____

Speech (cont.)

5. Read the excerpt from the speech and answer the question.

> Peaceable secession! Peaceable secession! The concurrent agreement of all the members of this great republic to separate? A voluntary separation, with alimony on one side and on the other! Why, what would be the result? Where is the line to be drawn? What States are to <u>secede</u>? What is to remain American? What am I to be? An American no longer?

Which word is **closest** in meaning to <u>secede</u> as it is used in the excerpt?
- ○ A. break away
- ○ B. divide equally
- ○ C. join together
- ○ D. take apart

6. In paragraph 2, Daniel Webster states, "Peaceable secession is an utter impossibility." What evidence does Webster provide in the speech to support his claim?

Write your answer in the box.

Name: _____ Date: _____

Autobiography

Directions: Read the text and answer the questions.

Text: *The Story of My Life* by Helen Keller

One day, while I was playing with my new doll, Miss Sullivan put my big rag doll into my lap also, spelled "d-o-l-l" and tried to make me understand that "d-o-l-l" applied to both. Earlier in the day we had had a tussle over the words "m-u-g" and "w-a-t-e-r." Miss Sullivan had tried to impress it upon me that "m-u-g" is mug and that "w-a-t-e-r" is water, but I persisted in confounding the two. In despair she had dropped the subject for the time, only to renew it at the first opportunity. I became impatient at her repeated attempts and, seizing the new doll, I dashed it upon the floor. I was keenly delighted when I felt the fragments of the broken doll at my feet. Neither sorrow nor regret followed my passionate outburst. I had not loved the doll. In the still, dark world in which I lived there was no strong sentiment or tenderness. I felt my teacher sweep the fragments to one side of the hearth, and I had a sense of satisfaction that the cause of my discomfort was removed. She brought me my hat, and I knew I was going out into the warm sunshine. This thought, if a wordless sensation may be called a thought, made me hop and skip with pleasure.

We walked down the path to the well-house, attracted by the fragrance of the honeysuckle with which it was covered. Some one was drawing water and my teacher placed my hand under the spout. As the cool stream gushed over one hand she spelled into the other the word *water*, first slowly, then rapidly. I stood still, my whole attention fixed upon the motions of her fingers. Suddenly I felt a misty consciousness as of something forgotten—a thrill of returning thought; and somehow the mystery of language was revealed to me. I knew then that "w-a-t-e-r" meant the wonderful cool something that was flowing over my hand. That living word awakened my soul, gave it light, hope, joy, set it free! There were barriers still, it is true, but barriers that could in time be swept away.

I left the well-house eager to learn. Everything had a name, and each name gave birth to a new thought. As we returned to the house every object which I touched seemed to quiver with life. That was because I saw everything with the strange, new sight that had come to me. On entering the door I remembered the doll I had broken. I felt my way to the hearth and picked up the pieces. I tried vainly to put them together. Then my eyes filled with tears; for I realized what I had done, and for the first time I felt repentance and sorrow.

I learned a great many new words that day. I do not remember what they all were; but I do know that *mother, father, sister, teacher* were among them—words that were to make the world blossom for me, "like Aaron's rod, with flowers." It would have been difficult to find a happier child than I was as I lay in my crib at the close of that eventful day and lived over the joys it had brought me, and for the first time longed for a new day to come.

Public Domain

Name: _____ Date: _____

Autobiography (cont.)

Assessment Questions

1. Why did Miss Sullivan finger spell words into Helen's hand?
   - ○ A. to teach Helen how to spell difficult words
   - ○ B. to explain to Helen the importance of words
   - ○ C. to demonstrate to Helen how to use sign language
   - ○ D. to help Helen connect words with objects

2. **Part A**
   Which phrase **best** describes the theme of the text?
   - ○ A. discovery of language
   - ○ B. price of loyalty
   - ○ C. building trust
   - ○ D. triumph over hardship

   Part B
   Which statement from the text **best** supports the answer in Part A?
   - ○ A. "In the still, dark world in which I lived there was no strong sentiment or tenderness."
   - ○ B. "Some one was drawing water and my teacher placed my hand under the spout."
   - ○ C. "Suddenly I felt a misty consciousness as of something forgotten—a thrill of returning thought; and somehow the mystery of language was revealed to me."
   - ○ D. "I learned a great many new words that day."

3. **Part A**
   Why did Helen throw her doll on the floor?
   - ○ A. She was excited about taking a walk in the sunshine.
   - ○ B. She was in a hurry to put on her hat.
   - ○ C. She became annoyed with Miss Sullivan's persistence.
   - ○ D. She wanted to get Miss Sullivan's attention.

   Part B
   Which sentence from the text supports the answer in Part A?
   - ○ A. "I became impatient at her repeated attempts and, seizing the new doll, I dashed it upon the floor."
   - ○ B. "Neither sorrow nor regret followed my passionate outburst."
   - ○ C. "I had not loved the doll."
   - ○ D. "Then my eyes filled with tears; for I realized what I had done, and for the first time I felt repentance and sorrow."

Name: _____ Date: _____

Autobiography (cont.)

4. Why did the author **most likely** write the text?
   - ○ A. to persuade readers to learn sign language
   - ○ B. to inform readers about an important event in her life
   - ○ C. to emphasize the importance of learning
   - ○ D. to explain to readers the important role of teachers

5. Read the excerpt and answer the question.

> I learned a great many new words that day. I do not remember what they all were; but I do know that *mother, father, sister, teacher* were among them—<u>words that were to make the world blossom for me</u>, "like Aaron's rod, with flowers."

What did Helen Keller **most likely** mean by the underlined phrase?
   - ○ A. Words made her silent world more bearable.
   - ○ B. Words helped her to communicate with her family.
   - ○ C. Words helped her emerge from a silent, dark world.
   - ○ D. Words made her world appear brighter.

6. Read the excerpt from the text and answer the question.

> On entering the door I remembered the doll I had broken. I felt my way to the hearth and picked up the pieces. I tried vainly to put them together. Then my eyes filled with tears; for I realized what I had done, and for the first time I felt <u>repentance</u> and sorrow.

Which word is a synonym for <u>repentance</u> as it is used in the sentence?
   - ○ A. grief
   - ○ B. pain
   - ○ C. regret
   - ○ D. shame

7. Which sentence describes the structure the author used to organize the text?
   - ○ A. The author describes events in the order in which they occur.
   - ○ B. The author presents a problem and gives a solution.
   - ○ C. The author compares important events in her life.
   - ○ D. The author states her point of view and supports it with details.

Name: _____ Date: _____

Autobiography (cont.)

8. Explain how the experience at the well-house changed Helen's life. Support your answer with details from the text.

Write your answer in the box.

Name: _____ Date: _____

Science Article

Directions: Read the text and answer the questions.

Text: "Wildlife Biologue: American Buffalo: (*Bison bison*)," November 1997

It is believed that buffalo, or bison, crossed over a land bridge that once connected the Asian and North American continents. Through the centuries buffalo slowly moved southward, eventually reaching as far south as Mexico and as far east as the Atlantic Coast, extending south to Florida. But the largest herds were found on the plains and prairies from the Rocky Mountains east to the Mississippi River, and from Great Slave Lake in Canada to Texas.

Because the great herds were nearly gone before any organized attempts were made to survey populations, we may never know just how many buffalo once roamed North America, although estimates range from 30 to 75 million. "The moving multitude ... darkened the whole plains," wrote Lewis and Clark, who encountered a herd at South Dakota's White River in 1806.

Although the buffalo's size and color, which ranges from light to dark brown, vary in different areas of the country, experts generally agree that all American buffalo belong to the same species. The differences in appearance probably result from the variety of environments in which they live.

Like their close relatives, domestic cattle and sheep, buffalo are cloven-hooved. Both males and females have a single set of hollow, curved horns. The male buffalo, called *bulls*, are immense, often weighing a ton or more and standing 5 to 6 feet high at the shoulders. The huge head and great hump covered with dark brown wooly hair contrast sharply with the relatively small hips. The females, or *cows*, are not as massive. Despite their great size and bulkiness, buffalo have amazing mobility, speed, and agility, and are able to sprint at speeds of up to 30 mph.

American Bison in North America

Year	Estimated Number
1500s	30,000,000–75,000,000
1889	2,000
1919	12,000
Present	500,000

In the spring, buffalo begin to shed their heavy winter coats, and soon their hair hangs in tatters. To hasten shedding and possibly to relieve their itching skin, buffalo rub against large stones and trees. By late spring, the only remaining long hairs are on the head, forelegs, and hump. To escape the torment of attacking insects, buffalo wallow in dust or sand.

With the arrival of the breeding season in mid- to late summer, the herds become restless. The bulls, aloof most of the year, now drift among the cows and calves. Noticeably quiet at other times, the bulls bellow hoarsely and become quarrelsome. Many fights occur over females, and the combatants, with lowered heads, paw the earth defiantly.

Name: _____ Date: _____

Science Article (cont.)

Cows give birth usually every year to one tawny to buff-colored calf. Most of the calves are born between the middle of April and end of May, but some arrive as late as October. At birth, the calves have only a faint suggestion of the hump they will develop later. Buffalo begin grazing (primarily on grasses) while still very young, although some may continue to nurse until they are nearly a year old. Buffalo may live to be about 20 years of age.

By 1800, the small buffalo herds east of the Mississippi River were gone. Buffalo may have been killed to protect livestock and farmlands in that region. With westward expansion of the American frontier, systematic reduction of the plains herds began around 1830, when buffalo hunting became the chief industry of the plains. Organized groups of hunters killed buffalo for hides and meat, often killing up to 250 buffalo a day.

Unfortunately, many people at the time also wanted to eradicate buffalo as a way to take away the livelihood and well-being of Native Americans. Native American tribes depended on the buffalo's meat and hides, and many still today believe the animal has special spiritual and healing powers, making it an important part of their culture.

The construction of the railroads across the plains further hastened the depletion of buffalo populations. Hunting from train windows was advertised widely and passengers shot them as the buffalo raced beside the trains. By 1883, both the northern and the southern herds had been destroyed. Less than 300 wild animals remained in the U.S. and Canada by the turn of the century out of the millions that once lived there.

Conservation of the buffalo came slowly. In May 1894, Congress enacted a law making buffalo hunting in Yellowstone National Park illegal. Eight years later, money was appropriated to purchase 21 buffalo from private herds to build up the Yellowstone herd. With adequate protection, this herd has steadily increased until it numbers almost 3,000 animals today. Hundreds of buffalo also inhabit the National Bison Range in the Flathead Valley of Montana, the Wichita Mountains National Wildlife Refuge in southwest Oklahoma, the Fort Niobrara National Wildlife Refuge in northern Nebraska, the Sullys Hill National Wildlife Refuge in northwestern North Dakota, and Walnut Creek National Wildlife Refuge in Central Iowa.

Many other private herds have boosted the buffalo's overall population over the years as well. While the present herds, numbering about 200,000 buffalo in all [in 1997], are not as large as the great herds that once ranged the North American continent, they are large enough to ensure the continued well-being of the American buffalo for generations to come.

Public Domain (U.S. Fish & Wildlife Service National Digital Library)

Name: _____ Date: _____

Science Article (cont.)

Assessment Questions

1. What is the central idea of the last two paragraphs of the text?
   ○ A. migration of the buffalo from Asia to North America
   ○ B. population trends of the North American buffalo
   ○ C. Westward Expansion of the American frontier
   ○ D. conservation efforts to save the North American buffalo

2. What is the author's **main** purpose for writing the text?
   ○ A. to persuade the reader to support American buffalo conservation programs
   ○ B. to explain to the reader the importance of the buffalo to Native Americans
   ○ C. to provide the reader with information about the American buffalo
   ○ D. to emphasize to the reader the importance of increasing the population of buffalo herds in North America

3. Based upon the text, what effect did westward expansion have on the population of American buffalo?
   ○ A. Westward expansion caused an increase in population.
   ○ B. Westward expansion caused a decrease in population.
   ○ C. Westward expansion had no effect on the population.
   ○ D. Westward expansion stabilized the population.

4. Which word **best** describes the tone of the passage?
   ○ A. reflective
   ○ B. judgmental
   ○ C. nostalgic
   ○ D. informative

5. Read the sentence from the text and answer the question.

> Unfortunately, many people at the time also wanted to <u>eradicate</u> buffalo as a way to take away the livelihood and well-being of Native Americans.

Which word is a synonym for <u>eradicate</u> as it is used in the sentence?
   ○ A. preserve
   ○ B. destroy
   ○ C. shelter
   ○ D. protect

Name: _____ Date: _____

Science Article (cont.)

6. Read the excerpt and answer the question.

> The construction of the railroads across the plains further hastened the depletion of buffalo populations. Hunting from train windows was advertised widely and passengers shot them as the buffalo raced beside the trains. By 1883, both the northern and the southern herds had been destroyed. Less than 300 wild animals remained in the U.S. and Canada by the turn of the century out of the millions that once lived there.

How does the author organize the information in the excerpt?
- ○ A. The cause and effect of an event is presented.
- ○ B. A main point is made and then supported by details.
- ○ C. Events are presented in chronological order.
- ○ D. Information is compared and contrasted.

7. How does the "American Bison in North America" chart **most likely** contribute to the understanding of the text?
- ○ A. The chart supports the idea that the bison population has drastically changed over time.
- ○ B. The chart illustrates the impact buffalo hunting had on the bison population.
- ○ C. The chart illustrates the impact railroads had on the bison population.
- ○ D. The chart supports the need for more federal legislation to protect the bison population.

8. Read the excerpt and answer the question.

> Because the great herds were nearly gone before any organized attempts were made to survey populations, we may never know just how many buffalo once roamed North America, although estimates range from 30 to 75 million. "The moving multitude ... darkened the whole plains," wrote Lewis and Clark, who encountered a herd at South Dakota's White River in 1806.

Why did the author **most likely** include the quote in the text?
- ○ A. to describe how the herd of buffalo looked moving across the plains
- ○ B. to reveal the location where Lewis and Clark saw the buffalo herd
- ○ C. to support the population estimates with an eyewitness account
- ○ D. to describe the location of buffalo herds in South Dakota in 1806

Science Article (cont.)

9. Which time of the year are calves **most likely** to be born?
   - ○ A. October
   - ○ B. May
   - ○ C. middle of April to end of May
   - ○ D. mid-to late summer

10. Based on the text, what were **four** major events that contributed to the near-extinction of the American buffalo? Use information from the text to support your answer.

    Write your answer in the box.

Name: _____ Date: _____

Newspaper Article

Directions: Read the text and answer the questions.

Text: "John Brown's Body," *New Bedford Mercury*—May 16, 1894.
New Bedford, Massachusetts

JOHN BROWN'S BODY

IT LIES MOLDERING IN A GRAVE AT NORTH ELBA, N.Y.

Many pilgrimages to the old John Brown farm in the picturesque Adirondacks region. The region has lately become a fashionable summer resort.

If the soul of John Brown is still marching on, as the old war song says, the grave in which the same mysteriously inspiring slogan hath it that his body lies moldering is becoming year by year a more interesting place of pilgrimage for students of his history and admirers of his deeds. It is yearly becoming more accessible, too, with the opening up and improvement of the roads and the building of railroads made necessary since the wild Adirondack region has become a fashionable summering place. The grave is situated on the farm which John Brown bought in 1849 from Gerrit Smith at North Elba, Essex County, N.Y., and only two miles distant from those beautiful twin lakes, Mirror and Placid, whereof "society" has lately become enamored.

A good road leads from Mirror lake to the John Brown farm, which is situated in the midst of the grandest scenery in the Adirondacks. It is an upland valley some 20 miles in length and of average breadth of 5 or 6 miles, and around it the forests have been cleared away for grazing farms, so that the country is opening up to present some charming sweeps of vision to the eye. To the north is the grand old Whiteface mountain, 4,000 feet in height, and from the farm one can look up its entire southern slope and see where it dips into the famous Wilmington notch.

Looking southward, the visitor has a magnificent view of the grandest of the Adirondack mountains. Mount Marcy, with its domelike crown piercing the atmosphere at an altitude of nearly 5,000 feet, is the highest mountain east of the Rockies with the single exception of Black mountain, in North Carolina. Near it is the Elephant, a long mountain with an apparent resemblance to the animal for which it is named. Westward of Marcy stands Mount McIntyre, second in height of the Adirondacks and affording, it is said, finer views than Marcy, owing to its more isolated position.

The finest views of all, however, are to be had from Whiteface, which also stands apart from the other mountains—seems, in fact, entirely separated from

Name: _____ Date: _____

Newspaper Article (cont.)

them. From its summit almost the entire length of Lake Champlain is visible as well as hundreds of the Adirondack lakes and the St. Laurence river. A project is now under consideration to make the summit of Whiteface more accessible. It is proposed to build a railroad up from Mirror lake, like those up Rigi and Pilatus in Switzerland and like those up Mount Washington and Pike's peak.

That John Brown must have had an inborn love of natural grandeur is shown by his selection of a burial place in the heart of this magnificent valley. But with his first coming to North Elba love of the beautiful had far less to do than his passionate love of freedom. What attracted him most was the fact that Gerrit Smith had there established a colony for Negroes rescued from slavery. It may be that he thought it would be a good center from which to propagate his openly avowed idea of organizing a Negro army to make war upon the slave holding states.

At any rate, he took a farm of 248 acres in the then unbroken wilderness, made a clearing and erected a little wooden house, which still stands where he built it, though it has been considerably improved in recent years. There he left his wife and the younger members of his family when he went to Kansas to fight against the extension of slavery into that territory. From there he went forth to his death on that famous raid on Harper's Ferry. There, after his execution, his wife took his body and buried it, in accordance with his desire in the shadow of a huge boulder that stands 30 or 40 feet away from the front of the house.

The house and farm are now the property of Kate Field, Sinclair Tousey, the sons of William Lloyd Garrison and several other admirers of John Brown. They bought the farm and put a neat wooden fence about the grave. Their aim was to protect the grave from desecration and farm from unworthy uses. The enclosure about the grave contains about an eighth of an acre and is filled with wild rosebushes. At the head of the grave stands a tombstone which John Brown brought from the grave of his grandfather at Torrington, Conn., and on it are inscriptions commemorative of his death and that of his three sons, who died, like him, in the effort to emancipate the negroes. The tombstone has to be kept boxed up and padlocked to protect it from desecration by relic hunters, who had already chipped it somewhat before this precaution was taken. The boulder has also suffered in like manner and has to be kept carefully guarded. On its summit, carved in great letters, is the inscription, "John Brown, 1859."

---

pilgrimage – journey to a special location

grandeur – the quality of being grand; splendor

propagate – to spread

Public Domain

Name: _____ Date: _____

Newspaper Article (cont.)

Assessment Questions

1. **Part A**
   Which statement **best** reflects the central idea of the text?
   ○ A. John Brown's grave site is a popular tourist attraction.
   ○ B. The Adirondack region is a popular vacation destination.
   ○ C. John Brown was against the extension of slavery to the Kansas territory.
   ○ D. Steps were taken to keep John Brown's grave safe from vandalism.

   Part B
   Which detail from the text **best** supports the answer in Part A?
   ○ A. "… the grave in which the same mysteriously inspiring slogan hath it that his body lies moldering is becoming year by year a more interesting place of pilgrimage for students of his history and admirers of his deeds."
   ○ B. "The grave is situated on the farm which John Brown bought in 1849 from Gerrit Smith at North Elba, Essex county, N.Y., and only two miles distant from those beautiful twin lakes, Mirror and Placid, whereof 'society' has lately become enamored."
   ○ C. "A good road leads from Mirror lake to the John Brown farm, which is situated in the midst of the grandest scenery in the Adirondacks."
   ○ D. "It is yearly becoming more accessible, too, with the opening up and improvement of the roads and the building of railroads made necessary since the wild Adirondack region has become a fashionable summering place."

2. Read the sentence from the text and answer the question.

   On its summit, carved in great letters, is the <u>inscription</u>, "John Brown, 1859."

   Which is the **best** synonym for the word <u>inscription</u> as it is used in the sentence?
   ○ A. caption
   ○ B. message
   ○ C. name
   ○ D. words

3. Which word describes the tone of the newspaper article?
   ○ A. comical
   ○ B. informative
   ○ C. friendly
   ○ D. concerned

Name: _____ Date: _____

Newspaper Article (cont.)

4. Which statement from the text is an opinion?
   - ○ A. "Looking southward, the visitor has a magnificent view of the grandest of the Adirondack mountains."
   - ○ B. "A project is now under consideration to make the summit of Whiteface more accessible."
   - ○ C. "There he left his wife and the younger members of his family when he went to Kansas to fight against the extension of slavery into that territory."
   - ○ D. "The enclosure about the grave contains about an eighth of an acre and is filled with wild rosebushes."

5. What factors contributed to the increase in tourism to John Brown's farm? Support your answer with textual evidence from the newspaper article.

   Write your answer in the box.

Name: _____ Date: _____

Flyer

Washington Middle School
Student Council Election

　　　Student council is a student-led organization that meets throughout the year. The purpose of student council is to provide leadership to the student body and promote school pride. Students who choose to run for the executive offices of President, Vice President, Secretary, Treasurer, and Historian will need to have special talents and characteristics to unite the students and encourage good citizenship at Washington Middle School.

　　　Interested students must complete the application forms and submit them to Mrs. Allen, Student Council Advisor, by September 27. All necessary forms and the application are available in the principal's office or online. Students filing for office must meet with Mrs. Allen after school on September 29 in Room 305. More details and information can be found online at <http://wms/studentcouncil/election.k12.us>.

Officer Responsibilities:
1. Attend all student council meetings.
2. Help coordinate, organize, and participate in school activities and events that promote school spirit.
3. Help coordinate, organize, and participate in school fundraisers.
4. Plan and work at school dances and activities.

Steps to Candidacy: (To be eligible, students must meet all requirements.)
1. Maintain a 3.0 GPA.
2. Complete and submit the student council application forms, including required essay.
3. Submit references from two of your present teachers.
4. Submit parent consent form.
5. Submit all paperwork to Mrs. Allen by September 27.

Campaign Dos:
1. All candidates must conduct a positive campaign.
2. Candidates may create three 8 ½" X 11" campaign posters. Posters can only be displayed in designated areas. All posters must be approved by Mrs. Allen.
3. Candidates will prepare a one- to three-minute campaign speech that presents a positive message. Speeches will be recorded before school on Wednesday, October 3, in the Technology Media Lab. Speeches will be shown to the student body on Friday, October 5, after morning announcements.

Campaign Don'ts:
1. Negative campaigning is forbidden.
2. Candidates may not distribute favors (e.g., candy and money).
3. Candidates are prohibited from making unreasonable campaign promises, such as no homework, shorter school days, and free ice cream on Fridays.
4. Candidates may not use social media for campaigning.

Name: _____ Date: _____

Flyer (cont.)

Assessment Questions

1. Read the sentence from the flyer and answer the question.

> Interested students must complete the application forms and <u>submit</u> them to Mrs. Allen, Student Council Advisor, by September 27.

   What is the **best** meaning of <u>submit</u> as it is used in the sentence?
   - ○ A. to carry
   - ○ B. to convey
   - ○ C. to deliver
   - ○ D. to mail

2. According to the flyer, what should a student do if they need more information about the election?
   - ○ A. ask the middle-school secretary
   - ○ B. contact the middle-school principal
   - ○ C. ask the student council advisor
   - ○ D. visit the online website

3. **Part A**
   Why does Mrs. Allen **most likely** have to approve all campaign posters?
   - ○ A. to prove that she is qualified to serve as student council advisor
   - ○ B. to make sure that all posters are student-created and not commercially produced
   - ○ C. to make sure all posters are the correct size and contain a positive message
   - ○ D. to inform the principal of any campaign misconduct

   Part B
   Select **two** details from the text that support your answer in Part A.
   - ○ A. "to provide leadership to the student body"
   - ○ B. "encourage good citizenship"
   - ○ C. "must conduct a positive campaign"
   - ○ D. "may create three 8 $\frac{1}{2}$" X 11" posters"
   - ○ E. "may not distribute favors"
   - ○ F. "may not use social media"

4. Based on the flyer, what will **most likely** happen if a candidate does not submit all forms to Mrs. Allen by September 27?
   - ○ A. The candidate will not be eligible to run for office.
   - ○ B. The candidate will not be allowed to use social media to campaign.
   - ○ C. The candidate will be required to meet with the principal.
   - ○ D. The candidate will be given an extension of 3 days.

Name: _____ Date: _____

Flyer (cont.)

5. When will the campaign speeches be shown to the middle-school student body?
   - ○ A. September 27
   - ○ B. September 29
   - ○ C. October 3
   - ○ D. October 5

6. What is the author's purpose for creating the flyer?
   - ○ A. to persuade students to run for a student council office
   - ○ B. to provide information about the student council election
   - ○ C. to describe the qualifications for becoming a candidate
   - ○ D. to emphasize the need for students to vote on election day

7. Which word **best** describes the tone of the flyer?
   - ○ A. formal
   - ○ B. friendly
   - ○ C. informative
   - ○ D. persuasive

8. What characteristics would a candidate **most likely** need in order to fulfill the responsibilities of an executive officer of the student council? Use textual evidence to support your answer.

   Write your answer in the box.

Name: _____ Date: _____

Paired Text

Directions: Read **Text One** and answer the questions.

Text One: *Eighty Years And More; Reminiscences 1815–1897* by Elizabeth Cady Stanton (Primary Source)

The general discontent I felt with woman's portion as wife, mother, housekeeper, physician, and spiritual guide, the chaotic conditions into which everything fell without her constant supervision, and the wearied, anxious look of the majority of women impressed me with a strong feeling that some active measures should be taken to remedy the wrongs of society in general, and of women in particular. My experience at the World's Anti-slavery Convention, all I had read of the legal status of women, and the oppression I saw everywhere, together swept across my soul, intensified now by many personal experiences. It seemed as if all the elements had conspired to impel me to some onward step. I could not see what to do or where to begin—my only thought was a public meeting for protest and discussion.

In this tempest-tossed condition of mind I received an invitation to spend the day with Lucretia Mott, at Richard Hunt's, in Waterloo. There I met several members of different families of Friends, earnest, thoughtful women. I poured out, that day, the torrent of my long-accumulating discontent, with such vehemence and indignation that I stirred myself, as well as the rest of the party, to do and dare anything. My discontent, according to Emerson, must have been healthy, for it moved us all to prompt action, and we decided, then and there, to call a "Woman's Rights Convention." We wrote the call that evening and published it in the *Seneca County Courier* the next day, the 14th of July, 1848, giving only five days' notice, as the convention was to be held on the 19th and 20th. The call was inserted without signatures,—in fact it was a mere announcement of a meeting,— but the chief movers and managers were Lucretia Mott, Mary Ann McClintock, Jane Hunt, Martha C. Wright, and myself. The convention, which was held two days in the Methodist Church, was in every way a grand success. The house was crowded at every session, the speaking good, and a religious earnestness dignified all the proceedings.

These were the hasty initiative steps of "the most momentous reform that had yet been launched on the world—the first organized protest against the injustice which had brooded for ages over the character and destiny of one-half the race." No words could express our astonishment on finding, a few days afterward, that what seemed to us so timely, so rational, and so sacred, should be a subject for sarcasm and ridicule to the entire press of the nation. With our Declaration of Rights and Resolutions for a text, it seemed as if every man who could wield a pen prepared a homily on "woman's sphere." All the journals from Maine to Texas seemed to strive with each other to see which could make our movement appear the most ridiculous. The anti-slavery papers stood by us manfully and so did Frederick Douglass, both in the convention and in his paper, *The North Star,* but so pronounced was the

Name: _____ Date: _____

Paired Text (cont.)

popular voice against us, in the parlor, press, and pulpit, that most of the ladies who had attended the convention and signed the declaration, one by one, withdrew their names and influence and joined our persecutors. Our friends gave us the cold shoulder and felt themselves disgraced by the whole proceeding.

If I had had the slightest premonition of all that was to follow that convention, I fear I should not have had the courage to risk it, and I must confess that it was with fear and trembling that I consented to attend another, one month afterward, in Rochester. Fortunately, the first one seemed to have drawn all the fire, and of the second but little was said. But we had set the ball in motion, and now, in quick succession, conventions were held in Ohio, Indiana, Massachusetts, Pennsylvania, and in the City of New York, and have been kept up nearly every year since.

Friends – also known as Quakers

torrent – an outpouring of words

premonition – forewarning

Public Domain

Assessment Questions

Use Text One, Eighty Years And More; Reminiscences 1815–1897, to answer questions 1-7.

1. **Part A**
   What is the central idea of the text?
   ○ A. Elizabeth Cady Stanton's involvement in the anti-slavery movement
   ○ B. Elizabeth Cady Stanton's involvement in the first Woman's Rights Convention
   ○ C. Declaration of Rights and Resolutions of July 1848
   ○ D. Frederick Douglass' support for the woman's rights movement

   Part B
   Select the sentence from the text that **best** supports the answer in Part A.
   ○ A. "I could not see what to do or where to begin—my only thought was a public meeting for protest and discussion."
   ○ B. "With our Declaration of Rights and Resolutions for a text, it seemed as if every man who could wield a pen prepared a homily on 'woman's sphere.'"
   ○ C. "The anti-slavery papers stood by us manfully and so did Frederick Douglass,... ."
   ○ D. "All the journals from Maine to Texas seemed to strive with each other to see which could make our movement appear the most ridiculous."

Name: _____ Date: _____

Paired Text (cont.)

2. Which word **best** describes the tone of the text?
   - ○ A. apprehensive
   - ○ B. hopeful
   - ○ C. reflective
   - ○ D. resentful

3. What is the author's purpose for writing the text?
   - ○ A. to persuade the reader to join the first organized women's protest
   - ○ B. to explain to the reader the author's anti-slavery beliefs
   - ○ C. to describe the public's reaction to the first women's convention
   - ○ D. to relate an important event in the author's life

4. Which point of view is used in the text?
   - ○ A. Elizabeth Cady Stanton reveals her own thoughts and feelings.
   - ○ B. Henry B. Stanton reveals his wife's thoughts and feelings.
   - ○ C. Elizabeth Cady Stanton's thoughts and feelings are revealed by Frederick Douglass.
   - ○ D. Lucretia Mott's thoughts and feelings are revealed by Elizabeth Cady Stanton.

5. Which statement from the text contains an opinion?
   - ○ A. "... I received an invitation to spend the day with Lucretia Mott, at Richard Hunt's, in Waterloo."
   - ○ B. "The convention, which was held two days in the Methodist Church, was in every way a grand success."
   - ○ C. "We wrote the call that evening and published it in the *Seneca County Courier*... ."
   - ○ D. "The call was inserted without signatures... ."

6. Which statement describes a reaction of the majority of women who attended the convention and signed the Declaration of Rights?
   - ○ A. The women attended a second convention in Rochester.
   - ○ B. The women submitted letters of support to *The North Star* newspaper.
   - ○ C. The women organized protest marches for women's rights.
   - ○ D. The women later withdrew their names from the declaration.

7. What is the author's purpose for including the first paragraph in the text?
   - ○ A. to explain the legal status of women in the 1800s
   - ○ B. to compare the Woman's Rights Convention to the World's Anti-slavery Convention
   - ○ C. to describe the role of women in the 1800s
   - ○ D. to provide an explanation for the author's decision to hold a public meeting concerning the rights of women

Name: _____ Date: _____

Paired Text (cont.)

Directions: Read **Text Two** and answer the questions.

Text Two: "Heroines of National Progress" by William H. Mace
(Secondary Source)

Elizabeth Cady Stanton, the First to Champion Woman Suffrage.

Elizabeth Cady was born at Johnstown, New York, in 1815. Her girlhood was a happy one, spent with her brother and sisters. She was a healthy, rosy-cheeked girl, full of life and fun. She believed girls were the equal of boys and had as much intellect as they had, and she would not allow boys to dictate to her.

When Elizabeth was eleven years old her brother died. Her father grieved deeply over the loss of his only son, and Elizabeth determined to try to be to her father all that her brother might have been. She therefore applied herself diligently to study and self-improvement.

Her father was a lawyer. He had been a member of Congress. Many hours out of school Elizabeth spent in his office, listening to his clients state their cases. She gradually became indignant at what she found to be the unequal position of women in almost every walk of life. She determined to devote her life to securing for women the same rights and privileges that men had.

While studying she did not neglect the arts of housekeeping. She regarded these as occupations of the highest dignity and importance. When twenty-five years old she married Henry B. Stanton, a lawyer and journalist who since his student days had talked and written against slavery. But she did not forget her old resolve to struggle for the rights of women, even when occupied with the duties of home and children.

The First Woman's Rights Convention.

In 1848 Mrs. Stanton called a woman's rights convention—the first ever held. Its purpose was "to discuss the social, civil, and religious conditions and rights of women."

Mrs. Stanton read to the convention a set of twelve resolutions, the now famous "Declaration of Sentiments." It demanded for women equality with men and "all the rights and privileges which belong to them as citizens of the United States," including the right to vote. This was the first public demand for woman suffrage. The resolutions were passed. A storm of ridicule followed the convention, but Mrs. Stanton's position remained unchanged.

Public Domain (*A Beginner's History* by William H. Mace, 1914)

Name: _____ Date: _____

Paired Text (cont.)

Assessment Questions

Use Text Two, "Heroines of National Progress," to answer questions 8–12.

8. Which event had the greatest impact on Elizabeth Cady Stanton's awareness of the inequality of women?
   ○ A. death of her brother
   ○ B. working in her father's law office
   ○ C. her marriage to Henry B. Stanton
   ○ D. becoming a mother

9. **Part A**
   What is the meaning of the word <u>suffrage</u> as it is used in the second paragraph of the text?
   ○ A. right to vote in public elections
   ○ B. equality for all women
   ○ C. resolutions passed at a convention
   ○ D. list of rights and privileges

   Part B
   Which phrase from the text helps the reader determine the meaning of the word <u>suffrage</u>?
   ○ A. "a set of twelve resolutions"
   ○ B. "demanded for women equality with men"
   ○ C. "the right to vote"
   ○ D. "a woman's rights convention"

10. What is the author's purpose for writing the text?
    ○ A. to persuade readers to join the women's suffrage movement
    ○ B. to explain the purpose of the "Declaration of Sentiments"
    ○ C. to inform readers about events surrounding the first woman's rights convention
    ○ D. to emphasize the importance of the twelve resolutions

11. Which word **best** describes the tone of the text?
    ○ A. sincere
    ○ B. judgmental
    ○ C. mocking
    ○ D. supportive

Name: _____ Date: _____

Paired Text (cont.)

12. What is the "Declaration of Sentiments"?
    ○ A. twelve resolutions passed by the woman's rights convention
    ○ B. letter to the convention from Mrs. Stanton
    ○ C. letter of support from the World's Anti-Slavery Convention
    ○ D. editorial written by Frederick Douglass

Assessment Questions

Use Text One and Text Two to answer question 13.

13. Read the claim from **Text Two** and answer the question.

> Mrs. Stanton read to the convention a set of twelve resolutions, the now famous "Declaration of Sentiments." It demanded for women equality with men and "all the rights and privileges which belong to them as citizens of the United States," including the right to vote. This was the first public demand for woman suffrage. The resolutions were passed. A storm of ridicule followed the convention, but Mrs. Stanton's position remained unchanged.

What textual evidence from **Text One** supports the claim that "Mrs. Stanton's position remained unchanged"?

Write your answer in the box.

Answer Keys

Instructional Resources

Reading Comprehension (p. 7)
>   Answer: C, D

Making Inferences (p. 8)
>   Answer: Part A: A; Part B: (response must include 2 of the possible answers) express riders carry news, messages, and copies of resolutions to other colonies; they sent Paul Revere from Boston to Lexington to warn Samuel Adams and John Hancock that the British were about to arrest them and to alert the militia that troops planned to seize weapons and ammunition stored at Concord.

Textual Evidence (p. 9)
>   Answer: (response must include 2 of the possible answers) "leading his country successfully through an arduous war"; his role in "establishing independence" for his country; being a leader during the "birth of a new government"; "scrupulously obeying the laws through his whole career"; an acquaintance of 30 years

Theme (p. 10)
>   Answer: Part A: B; Part B: *But in my sleep to you I fly: / I'm always with you in my sleep!*

Central Idea (p.11)
>   Answer: A, F

Summary (p. 12)
>   Answer: A, E

Word Meaning (p. 13)
>   Answer: C, F

Tone (p. 14)
>   Answer: Part A: D; Part B: (response must include 2 of the possible answers): a cheer began to grow and grow, which burst into a roar as he passed the firewood and halted at command; hats and mittens were flying in the air; men were shaking hands; bubbling over in a general incoherent babel

Organizational Text Structures (p. 15)
>   Answer: D

Author's Purpose (p. 16)
>   Answer: C

Point of View (p. 17)
>   Answer: D

Practice Assessments
Literature

Novel (p. 20)
>   1. B;
>   2. D or F; If D is chosen in Part A, the answer is A and D in Part B. If F is chosen in Part A, the answer is C and E in Part B.;
>   3. C; 4. B; 5. B, D, and G; 6. D; 7. B; 8. C, F; 9. A; 10. A
>   11. In Excerpt 1, Archibald Craven recognizes that a change has come over him. He doesn't recognize what has happened to him, but he feels as though something has been "unbound and released in him." He responds to his feelings with the words, "I almost feel as if—I were alive!". Excerpt 2 helps the reader

understand that the change in Craven described in Excerpt 1 happened at the same time as Colin's experience in the secret garden, when he cries out "I am going to live forever and ever and ever!" This shows a strong connection between Craven and Colin.

Poem (p. 24)
1. C, D; 2. A; 3. B; C; 4. A; 5. D; 6. D; 7. B; 8. D; A, B, C
9. In stanza one and two, the tone is sad and mournful. In stanza one, the speaker complains about how the weather makes the day "dark and dreary." In stanza two, the speaker compares his life to the "dark and dreary" day. He is getting older, but instead of looking forward to tomorrow, he allows his thoughts to "cling to the mouldering past." In stanza three, the tone changes to renewed hope. The speaker tells himself to quit being sad, and "cease repining" on lost youth. He finally realizes that even though the day may be "dark and dreary" now, he can still have hope that afterwards, the sun will shine. He realizes that aging "is the common fate of all," and there is renewed hope that in the future only "some days must be dark and dreary."

Drama (p. 30)
1. B; 2. A; 3. C; 4. B; 5. A; 6. D; 7. D; 8. D
9. (Answers will vary but may include) Alice is curious, because "she picks up a book" that she has never seen before and looks inside. Alice is polite, because she didn't want to "refuse" the Red Queen's offer of a biscuit, even though she was thirsty. When she "curtseys as she takes the biscuit" she is showing that she is respectful.

Informational Text
Speech (p. 36)
1. D; B, D; 2. C; 3. B; 4. A; 5. A
6. To support his claim that peaceable succession is impossible, Daniel Webster uses rhetorical questions to present the problems that would occur with succession. These questions were: "Where is the line to be drawn?"; "What States are to secede?"; "What is to remain American?"; "What am I to be? An American no longer?"; "Where is the flag of the republic to remain?"; "What is to become of the army?"; "What is to become of the navy?"; "What is to become of the public lands?"; and "How is each of the thirty States to defend itself?". Trying to come to an agreement on these issues would make peaceable succession impossible.

Autobiography (p. 39)
1. D; 2. A; C; 3. C; A; 4. B; 5. C; 6. C; 7. A
8. Before the incident at the well-house, Helen was a child who lived in a dark world and felt "no strong sentiment or tenderness." She was impatient with learning and unable to differentiate between the meaning of words such as "mug'" and "water." Helen stated that, "I persisted in confounding the two." When Mrs. Sullivan took her to the well-house, she put Helen's hand under the water spout. As the water "gushed over one hand" Mrs. Sullivan spelled the word water into the other hand. This was Helen's "eureka" moment. The "living word awakened" her soul and gave it "light, hope, joy and set it free." The "mystery of language" was now revealed to her. After this incident, she was happier and "eager to learn." For the first time, she felt "repentance and sorrow" and looked forward "for a new day to come."

Science Article (p. 44)
1. D; 2. C; 3. B; 4. D; 5. B; 6. A; 7. A; 8. C; 9. C
10. The four major events that contributed to the near extinction of the American buffalo population were "westward expansion of the American frontier," the industry of buffalo hunting, the eradication of "buffalo as a way to take away the livelihood and well-being of Native Americans," and the railroad construction.

Newspaper Article (p. 49)
1. A; A; 2. D; 3. B; 4. A
5. (Answers will vary but may include) There are several factors that contributed to the increase in tourism to John Brown's farm. The improvement of roads in the Adirondack region made it easier "for students of his history and admirers of his deeds" to make the pilgrimage to the farm. The building of railroads opened up the "wild Adirondack region" and turned it into "a fashionable summering place" for tourists. Mirror and Placid Lakes were popular tourist destinations, and John Brown's grave site was only two miles from the lakes. Also, the farm was situated in an isolated "upland valley" where tourists could view some of "the grandest scenery in the Adirondacks."

Flyer (Functional Text) (p. 52)
1. C; 2. D; 3. C; C, D; 4. A; 5. D; 6. B; 7. C
8. (Answers will vary but must be supported with textual evidence.)

Paired Text
Text One (p. 55)
1. B; A; 2. C; 3. D; 4. A; 5. B; 6. D; 7. D
Text Two (p. 58)
8. B; 9. A; C; 10. C; 11. A; 12. A
Text One and Text Two (p. 59)
13. A few days after the convention, the majority of people ridiculed the event; however, Mrs. Stanton's position remained unchanged. Mrs. Stanton did not withdraw her name from the declaration as did a majority "of ladies who had attended the convention and signed the declaration". Unlike those ladies, she did not join the "persecutors." Even though she confessed "that it was with fear and trembling," she agreed to attend another convention, one month later, in Rochester.